# KINDLINGS

*poems by*

# Rachel Linnea Brown

*Finishing Line Press*
Georgetown, Kentucky

# KINDLINGS

Copyright © 2026 by Rachel Linnea Brown
ISBN 979-8-89990-349-6 First Edition
All rights reserved under International and Pan-American Copyright Conventions. No part of this book may be reproduced in any manner whatsoever without written permission from the publisher, except in the case of brief quotations embodied in critical articles and reviews.

## ACKNOWLEDGMENTS

Many thanks to my husband, chocolate Labradors, family, and friends for their indefatigable hope. There's no place like home.

I will forever admire and appreciate my students. You invite me to grow, you listen, and you inspire.

Teachers and mentors—past and present—mean more than you will ever know.

Thank you to the flora and fauna of present-day Indiana, Wisconsin, and Kansas. Your solace and resilience infuse this collection.

With affection for my journal. You held just enough pages to safely deliver us.

Publisher: Leah Huete de Maines
Editor: Christen Kincaid
Cover Art: Rachel Linnea Brown
Illustrations: Rachel Linnea Brown
Author Photo: Matthew T. Bristow
Cover Design: Elizabeth Maines McCleavy

Order online: www.finishinglinepress.com
also available on amazon.com

Author inquiries and mail orders:
Finishing Line Press
PO Box 1626
Georgetown, Kentucky 40324
USA

# Contents

"clear blue" ............................................................. 1
"dread shut" ........................................................... 2
"break" .................................................................... 3
"incandescent" ....................................................... 4
"delicate untended thing" .................................... 5
"let me write about burning" ............................... 6
"balm" ..................................................................... 7
"sweet-mown" ........................................................ 9
"east 19 mph" ....................................................... 10
"soar" ..................................................................... 11
"old growth" .......................................................... 12
"coy" ...................................................................... 13
"berth" ................................................................... 15
"anniversary poem" ............................................. 17
"curious girl" ........................................................ 18
"whole" .................................................................. 19
"july" ...................................................................... 20
"goodbye poem" ................................................... 21
"release" ................................................................ 22
"slip from the pages" .......................................... 23
"waiting" ............................................................... 24
"unsung" ............................................................... 25
"settle" ................................................................... 26
"poised" ................................................................. 28
"ambient" .............................................................. 29
"poised" ................................................................. 30
"missing poem" .................................................... 31
"return poem" ...................................................... 32

*With love and gratitude to all who tended the flame:*

Matt Bristow, Beamish Chillicothe, Lindy Indy Ann, Baby Brown, Deana and Kevin Brown, Pam and Ed Bristow, Jennifer Allison, Angela Cloud, Cynthia White, Hannah Peterson, Tara Glore, Kelly Edmondson, Joy Polson, and Laura Mielke.

**"CLEAR BLUE"**

uncertain page     dotted
with longing.

## "DREAD SHUT"

incapable of listing

wake

listening

between what can

and what will

be

unwelled.

## "BREAK"

how
sandy the soil
and how shallow
the roots
of the page
curling
between pleasant
dark
and something
warmer
no
thought of being
enough
no
guide or obligation
unmet
simultaneously
listening
and not
responsive
to minor
threat.

## "INCANDESCENT"

like a web at sunset
poised
to catch any unwitting
seed or insect.
is there
something more to feel
or do?
I brush one thread
and everything
shivers
blend breath
and gust
as though I belong
restless
yet barely effective
tending
another slow
burn.

## "DELICATE UNTENDED THING"

brave
enough to unfurl
bend
a little
in the sun
bleed
enough to confirm
life
without course
nod
along to whatever
rustles
or bereaves
wise
enough to avoid
white
flickering
heat.

## "LET ME WRITE ABOUT BURNING"

hurl

words

at this vessel

as though it will catch

every white

curl

and wink out

without

scar.

"BALM"

I didn't
expect your evening
softness, palm to palm
with oak
ridges
and billowing
orange, pink, and blue
stars
blinking gently
as fireflies
rose
around us
without care for anything
except each
other
and superfluous words
settling
softly on our
skin.

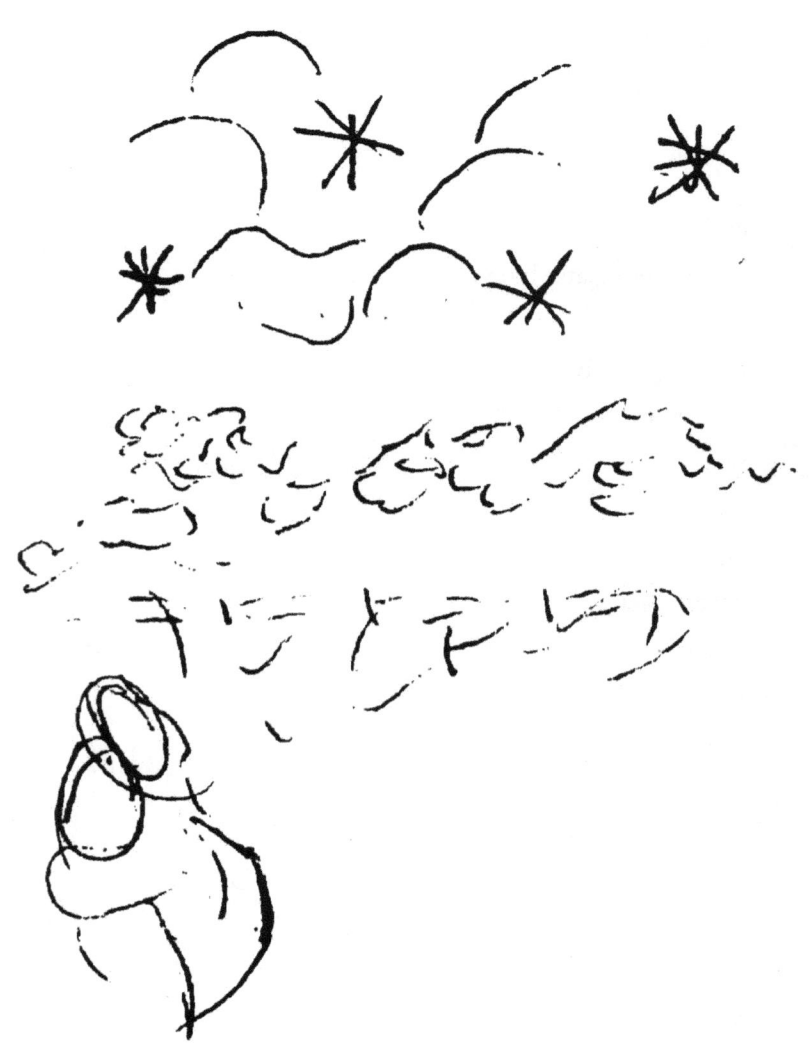

**"SWEET-MOWN"**

subsume
into full-throated
June
wild fruit
plumping upon
stems.

## "EAST 19 MPH"

I
brace
my letters
as though I
should
be
all strength all
at once
not
anxious
in the lulls
for what might
come next
and from which
direction.
hold
your ground as you
know
it,
hardy
little thing.

## "SOAR"

a spider drops
upon
my page.
I am
mercy.
another follows
soon after
and
I am
reluctant
path,
meandered.
wind fresh-
stirs
the white birch
limbs
and drives
the rain, disturbed.
your storm
hasn't drummed
my chest
yet.
I
might not
fully
rend your
sky.

**"OLD GROWTH"**

what
ground
was this once
but a monument
without
sole.

## "COY"

I
stretch
side-
ways and upside
down
and sometimes
merge
over years
to thwart and attract
you,
flex delicate veins,
withhold the right
phrase,
and bear
the cardinal weight
of wind
and lichen.

## "BERTH"

we
approach
as though we should
ask
permission,
surprised by the northern blue
flag
at the end of its season
and heart-round
lilies
bobbing
upon ponderous
stems.
everything
is as it should be
without
us.
curious,
we advance.
red wings critique
our path
and loons sink
deeper into nest
hoping we will pass,
harmless.
we are courteous.
we

drift against
a consequent bank,
silence.
beavers rearrange
limbs
to bleach in years
and ignore
us
like always, a thousand
fires
a thousand miles
away
scattering
sun.

## "ANNIVERSARY POEM"

our
illusion didn't stop
time
but slowed it so
the shadows that crept
across the leaves
and
the birds
that sang between
the shadows
barely
knew we breathed.

## "CURIOUS GIRL"

I
was a stone
upon
shore smoothed
by grains
          pushed
     and pulled
by moon
and dried by sun
as soon
       as wetted
when you wondered
     how do I reveal
and withdraw
again
         so quickly
and where will I
go
when you discover
the next
remarkable     thing?

**"WHOLE"**

the blackbird on the track
might
be a poem looking
at nothing
we expect, unfurled
on a whim
or bundled for
oblivion,
distinguished
only
by an eye.

## "JULY"

one thread
links
pebble and star.
say
nothing and save
only
the scrap you intend
to ignite.
coyotes
and fireflies cavort
in the close-enough
dark.
all might be
well
without us.

**"GOODBYE POEM"**

unfurl
your loftiest
towers
and throatiest
cores
as though you could offer
an ambitious
sky
and depth
for the lettered
wanderer
longing for home.

**"RELEASE"**

who
will spindle
        sorrow
into future    worthy
of moth?

## "SLIP FROM THE PAGES"

what license
do you require
to release
another year's
hopes
and regrets,
loves
imperfectly
expressed, no
apologies
to trim
and press into
pages
and forget
until we are bored,
curious,
or on the move
again
and we
disturb the old
words?

## "WAITING"

distill
light into truth
worthy
of page. what
page
could bear
you?
you
know we burn
but not
how
we will distinguish
smoke
from cloud.

**"UNSUNG"**

offer
no truth
      heavier
than sunlight
in rain.

## "SETTLE"

let
one daisy
infiltrate the field
and
coneflowers might
choke.
*
I
dare
you to imagine
what might happen
when this poem
thrives
and its limbs
pierce your uncertain
black sky.
you will never
return.
*
your
sadness rustles
or stagnates
without
reason. you will
suffer
as you allow.
*

love self
into self.
I
soften
the edge of all
you
will feel
for now, cutting
stems.

## "POISED"

I
am
an almighty
dam's
first trickle.
observe
at your own
peril.

"AMBIENT"

will
you risk staring
straight
on?
draw
your tightly pressed
hopes
across this raw
page.
no
one else will
burn.

## "POISED"

let's escape
gently,
like sunlight on a still
evening,
namelessly blue
receding
as robins and finches
converse
about the stability
of nests.

## "MISSING POEM"

I
loved you
into limestone
ridges
and seedy hopes
scattered
into stranger
valleys.
this
is where the flood
will glisten.
parallel receding
clouds trail
our stalwart, transitional
selves.
let
nothing else
well.

"RETURN POEM"

I
gathered
nothing more
    in the end
than each granular
hope returning
to shore.

Rachel Linnea Brown earned her PhD in American literature from the University of Kansas (2019), her MFA in poetry from Colorado State University (2014), and her BA in English from the University of Central Missouri (2011). She is an Instructor of English at Haskell Indian Nations University, where she teaches poetry writing, creative writing, introduction to literature, and composition.

Rachel's scholarly essays have appeared in *Studies in American Indian Literatures* and *American Contact: Intercultural Encounter and the Boundaries of Book History*, and her creative work has circulated in journals such as *Gulf Coast, Black Warrior Review, Midwest Quarterly, Subtropics,* and *South Dakota Review*. *Kindlings* is her debut collection.

Beyond academia, Rachel enjoys engaging with local history, geology, and ecology. In addition to restoring their circa 1858 limestone farmhouse, Rachel and her husband have planted a thirty-tree orchard; cultivated heirloom irises, lilacs, peonies, and persimmons; collected fossils and red quartzite stones from their meadows (deposited in present-day Kansas by glaciers during the last ice age); and preserved fifteen acres of untilled prairie. Beamish and Lindy, chocolate Labradors extraordinaire, love swimming in "The Branch" and running through the tall grass. The best days close with stargazing and a song.

www.ingramcontent.com/pod-product-compliance
Lightning Source LLC
Chambersburg PA
CBHW030051100426
42734CB00038B/1218